DISASTERS
PEOPLE IN PERIL

UNSINKABLE!
THE TITANIC SHIPWRECK

Michael D. Cole

Enslow Publishers, Inc.
40 Industrial Road
Box 398
Berkeley Heights, NJ 07922
USA
http://www.enslow.com

Original edition published as *The* Titanic*: Disaster at Sea* in 2001.

Library of Congress Cataloging-in-Publication Data
Cole, Michael D.
Unsinkable! : the Titanic shipwreck / Michael D. Cole.
p. cm. — (Disasters—people in peril)
Includes bibliographical references and index.
Summary: "Explores the tragic disaster of the *Titanic*, including the construction of the massive ship, the shipwreck on its maiden voyage, stories from survivors, and its legacy in history"—Provided by publisher.
ISBN 978-0-7660-4017-5
1. Titanic (Steamship)—Juvenile literature. 2. Shipwrecks—North Atantic Ocean—Juvenile literature. I. Title.
G530.T6C663 2013
910.9163'4—dc23
2012001408

Future editions:
Paperback ISBN 978-1-4644-0106-0
ePUB ISBN 978-1-4645-1013-7
PDF ISBN 978-1-4646-1013-4

Printed in the United States of America

032012 Lake Book Manufacturing, Inc., Melrose Park, IL

10 9 8 7 6 5 4 3 2 1

To Our Readers: We have done our best to make sure all Internet addresses in this book were active and appropriate when we went to press. However, the author and the publisher have no control over and assume no liability for the material available on those Internet sites or on other Web sites they may link to. Any comments or suggestions can be sent by e-mail to comments@enslow.com or to the address on the back cover.

Enslow Publishers, Inc., is committed to printing our books on recycled paper. The paper in every book contains 10% to 30% post-consumer waste (PCW). The cover board on the outside of each book contains 100% PCW. Our goal is to do our part to help young people and the environment too!

Illustration Credits: AP Images, p. 7; AP Images / Ralph White, p. 41; AP Images / Tom Gannam, p. 42; The Granger Collection, NYC, pp. 4, 16, 18, 23, 31; Library of Congress Prints and Photographs, pp. 11, 13, 14, 20, 26, 33; National Archives and Records Administration, p. 28; Public Domain Image, 1912, p. 6; © The Star-Ledger / Patti Sapone / The Image Works, p. 36; 20th Century Fox / Paramount / The Kobal Collection / Wallace, Merie W., p. 39; ullstein bild / The Granger Collection, pp. 1, 8.

Cover Illustration: ullstein bild / The Granger Collection, NYC (Painting by Willy Stöwer of the sinking of the *Titanic* on April 14–15, 1912).

CONTENTS

Shortly after midnight on April 15, 1912, Harold Cottam, the wireless communication operator on the *Carpathia*, received a distress call from the RMS *Titanic*. The great ship had struck an iceberg and was sinking fast.

CHAPTER ONE

"ICEBERG RIGHT AHEAD!"

IT WAS 12:15 A.M. ON APRIL 15, 1912. Harold Cottam was operating the wireless communication system aboard the steamer ship *Carpathia*. Cottam was almost done with his shift when a series of Morse code messages started to come through. He quickly sat down to decode them.

"Require immediate assistance. . . . Come at once. . . . We have struck an iceberg . . . sinking." The message was followed by the location of the ship and the letters CQD, which meant "Come, Quick, Danger." The message also included the letters MGY.[1]

Cottam was shocked. The letters MGY were the code symbols for the RMS *Titanic*.

Newspapers around the world had been filled with stories about the *Titanic* as it prepared for its maiden voyage across the Atlantic Ocean, from England to New York. The *Titanic* was the largest ocean liner ever built. Its engineering and design were state-of-the-art. Builders believed the mighty ship was virtually unsinkable.

Before the ship's maiden voyage and tragic disaster, the White Star Line advertised the *Titanic*'s one-of-a-kind qualities, including luxuries never seen before on a ship.

The *Titanic* had departed from Southampton, England, five days earlier on April 10, 1912. After brief stops in France and Ireland to pick up more passengers, the *Titanic* steamed out to sea. More than two thousand passengers and crew were aboard.

Cottam quickly informed his captain of the message he had just heard. Fifty-eight miles away, the *Titanic* was sinking.

Aboard the doomed ship, little more than half an hour had passed since lookout Frederick Fleet had spotted a dark mass in the distance.

"Iceberg right ahead," Fleet had quickly warned the officers on the bridge. However, the giant ship had not turned in time and scraped the side of the iceberg. In a matter of seconds, the ship's fate had been sealed. The iceberg had opened the *Titanic*'s hull. Water flooded into the forward compartments.[2]

In the crow's nest, lookout Frederick Fleet spotted an iceberg in the distance, warning the ship's officers on the bridge. But the warning did not give the ship enough time to turn and avoid it. This is a photo of the *Titanic* taken in 1912 as it steamed out to sea.

This painting by Willy Stöwer shows passengers and crew members rowing lifeboats away from the *Titanic* as it sinks into the ocean.

The terrible news then spread to the crew and passengers. The *Titanic* had struck an iceberg and was going down. Stewards moved quickly across the ship's many decks. Passengers were told to get to the lifeboat deck and put on their lifejackets. For the next two hours, a tragic drama would unfold upon the decks of the *Titanic*. The ill-fated ship and its passengers were about to slip into history.

Even before its maiden voyage, the *Titanic* had become a kind of symbol. Its great size and luxury represented the best that could be produced with that era's wealth and know-how. People of all classes, from the very rich to the very poor, were aboard the ship that night. The loss of so many lives aboard the *Titanic* made the ship's sinking a great tragedy.

The *Titanic* began as a triumph of the human spirit. It represented the human desire to build things bigger and better. Its end would be a reminder that nothing on the sea is unsinkable and that nothing in the world is certain.

CHAPTER TWO

THE BIGGEST AND FINEST

IN THE EARLY TWENTIETH CENTURY, traveling was much different than it is today. There was no air travel for regular passengers. Airplanes had just been invented. Travel by ship was rough. Crossing the Atlantic sometimes meant week-long voyages aboard ships. Conditions were usually not comfortable or relaxing.

The British owners and builders of the White Star Line of ships had been trying to change the style of sea travel since 1870. In that year, the White Star Line launched its first ship, the *Oceanic*. It had many features that made travel more comfortable for passengers. The company built five other ocean liners between 1899 and 1907. Each one set a new record for size.

By 1909, the technology existed not only to build the ships larger, but also to fit them with engines that were faster and more reliable. The White Star Line set out to build a new fleet of liners of extreme luxury to appeal to the world's wealthiest travelers. J. Bruce Ismay, manager

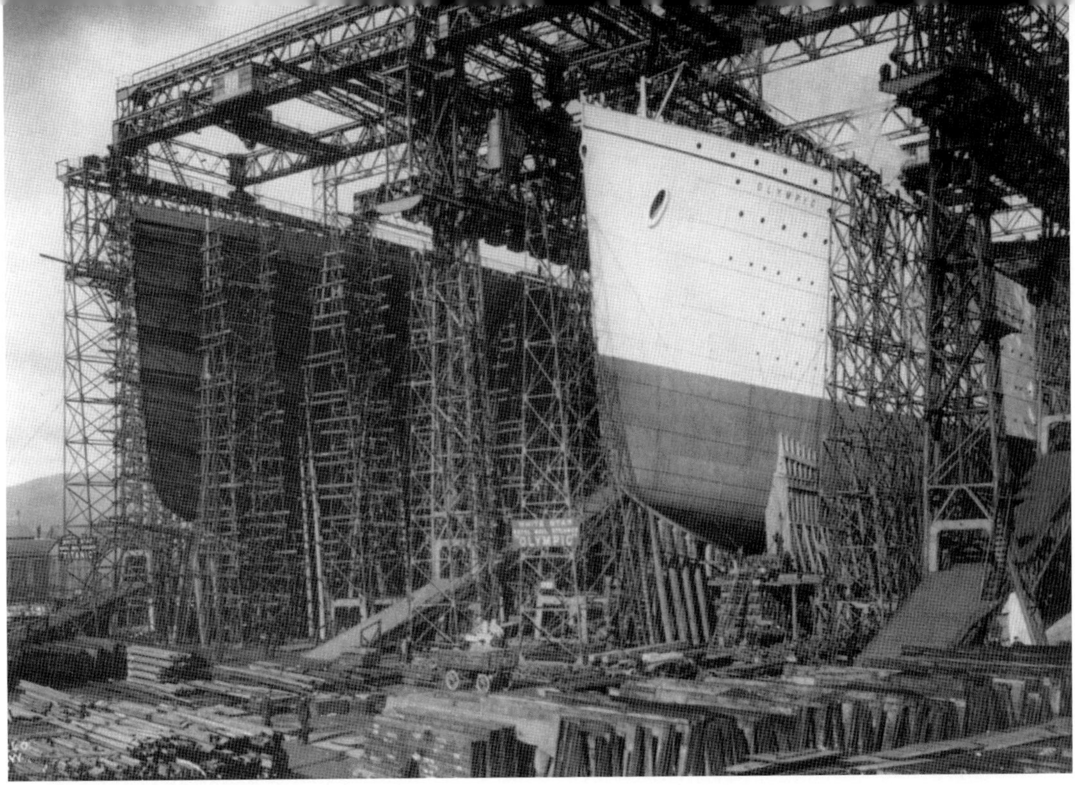

Owners of the White Star Line wanted to change the style of sea travel by creating larger and faster ships while also providing comfort and luxury for its passengers. In 1909, they began to build three ships for the wealthiest travelers. This photo shows the bows of the *Olympic* (right) and the *Titanic* (left) during construction between 1909 and 1911 in Belfast, Ireland.

of the White Star Line, wanted to build three ships—the *Olympic,* the *Titanic,* and the *Gigantic.* The *Olympic* was built first and successfully launched in October 1910. But the *Titanic* was to be even bigger and more luxurious.[1]

Construction on the hull of the *Titanic* began in March 1909 at the shipyard of the Harland and Wolff shipbuilding firm in Belfast, Ireland. The *Titanic*'s hull was 882 feet long, nearly the length of three football fields. The design included nine decks, making the ship as tall as an eleven-story building. It was driven by three giant steam engines, which were powered by twenty-nine boilers. Each boiler was fifteen feet high and weighed more than one hundred tons. When completed, the ship contained twenty-five thousand tons of steel, held together by more than 3 million rivets.[2]

An important part of the ship's design was the sixteen separate watertight compartments in the hull. If a collision were to rip a hole anywhere in the hull, the compartments would then be sealed off by giant iron doors. Sealing off the area that was taking on water would keep the water from spreading through the rest of the ship. Even if three of the sixteen compartments became completely filled with water, the ship would still stay afloat. No one ever imagined a collision would occur that could damage three compartments.

"I cannot conceive of any vital disaster happening to this vessel," said Captain Edward Smith after taking command of the *Titanic*. "Modern shipbuilding has gone beyond that." After a long and successful career at sea, Captain Smith had been scheduled to take the *Titanic*'s maiden voyage as his last command before retiring. Captain Smith would carry out his duties to the end, but he would not retire.[3]

The *Titanic*'s giant hull was launched on May 31, 1911. The rest of its structure, including the many cabins, restaurants, saloons, lounges, and even a gym, were completed later as the ship remained secured at dry dock. A dry dock is a structure that holds a ship in place while it is completed or repaired. No expense was spared in the decoration of the first- and second-class passengers' suites. Their furnishings included

Members of a work crew stand under one of the *Titanic*'s large engine propellers on May 31, 1911, the day the hull was launched.

more than thirty different kinds of chairs, fifty varieties of tables, oak beds, brass beds, and electric heaters. Some of the rooms had elaborate oak paneling and a fireplace.

When the *Titanic* was completed in April 1912, it performed beautifully in sea trials. Then builders signed papers that turned ownership of the *Titanic* over to the White Star Line. Publicity describing the ship's tremendous size and design generated a great deal of public interest.

First-class passengers enjoyed extravagant luxuries aboard the *Titanic*. Elaborate private rooms, a Turkish bath, and a gym were just some of the amenities. The photo at left shows the main dining room on the saloon deck and the photo below shows the wide promenade deck.

A 1911 edition of the magazine *Shipbuilder* described how the ship's special watertight doors would save the *Titanic* in case of collision at sea.

"The Captain may, by simply moving an electric switch, instantly close the doors throughout and make the vessel practically unsinkable," one writer claimed.[4] Many similar claims that the huge ship was unsinkable appeared in other magazines and newspapers.

The ship's maiden voyage would leave port from Southampton, England, on April 10, 1912. The passenger list for this voyage included some of the richest and most famous people in the world. This created even more public interest in the ship.[5]

Wealthy American industrialist Benjamin Guggenheim would be aboard. Isidor Straus, founder of the world-famous Macy's department store in New York City, was traveling with his wife. John Jacob Astor IV, the wealthy great-grandson of the famous American fur trader, would also be on board. Margaret Brown, the wife of Denver millionaire James J. Brown, would be traveling without her husband aboard the *Titanic*. Known to her friends as "Molly," Brown's actions during the *Titanic*'s sinking would become legendary.

More than half of the ship's passengers were traveling in third class. Passage aboard this part of the ship was inexpensive. The third-class areas had none of the luxuries or comforts enjoyed by passengers on the upper decks. Many of these third-class passengers were immigrants from Europe. They were making their way across the Atlantic Ocean to start a new life in the United States.[6]

At noon on April 10, 1912, with great fanfare, the *Titanic* pulled away from the dock at Southampton, England. The British crew numbered 892. They included the men in the engineering rooms, the stewards, cooks, waiters, and storekeepers, and the officers on the bridge. On this first voyage of the giant new ship, the White Star Line's president, J. Bruce Ismay, was aboard to observe. Thomas Andrews, the chief designer of the *Titanic*, was also onboard to see how the ship performed, both at sea and at providing comfort and amusement to its passengers.

R.M.S. "TITANIC"

APRIL 14, 1912

FIRST CLASS DINNER

HORS D'OEUVRE VARIES

OYSTERS

CONSOMME OLGA — CREAM OF BARLEY

SALMON, MOUSSELINE SAUCE, CUCUMBER

FILET MIGNONS LILI

SAUTE OF CHICKEN LYONNAISE

VEGETABLE MARROW FARCIE

LAMB, MINT SAUCE

ROAST DUCKLING, APPLE SAUCE

SIRLOIN OF BEEF — CHATEAU POTATOES

GREEN PEAS — CREAMED CARROTS

BOILED RICE

PARMENTIER & BOILED NEW POTATOES

PUNCH ROMAINE

ROAST SQUAB & CRESS

RED BURGUNDY

COLD ASPARAGUS — VINAIGRETTE

PATE DE FOIE GRAS

CELERY

WALDORF PUDDING

PEACHES IN CHARTREUSE JELLY

CHOCOLATE & VANILLA ECLAIRS

FRENCH ICE CREAM

On April 10, 1912, the *Titanic* left port from Southampton, England. For the next three days, passengers enjoyed the many offerings of the remarkable ship. This is a first-class dinner menu from April 14, 1912.

The *Titanic* crossed the English Channel and stopped twice to take on additional passengers. First it stopped at Cherbourg, France, and then at Queenstown, Ireland. When the ship steamed away from Ireland on the afternoon of April 11, the official count was 1,316 passengers and 892 crew, for a total of 2,208 aboard. Passengers enjoyed themselves for the next three days and nights aboard the lavish ship.

The *Titanic* was equipped with a wireless communication system, an early form of radio. Radio voice communication had not yet been developed, so wireless operators sent and received messages tapped out in Morse code. On April 14, the *Titanic*'s wireless operators began receiving a number of iceberg warnings from other ships. Despite the warnings, Captain Smith gave orders for an increase in speed. He pushed the ship to 22½ knots (about 23 miles per hour). Other ice warnings continued to come in.[7]

At 11:40 P.M., lookouts Frederick Fleet and Reginald Lee were struggling to stay warm in the ship's crow's nest. The crow's nest is a lookout tower near the front of a ship. There, two sailors could scan the sea ahead of the ship to make sure the way was clear. Mist moving across the water was making their job even more difficult.

Suddenly, Fleet spotted a dark mass in the distance directly ahead of the ship. He quickly rang the alarm bell three times. Then he grabbed the telephone to give the duty officer on the bridge an urgent report.

"Are you there?" Fleet asked.

"Yes," the officer responded. "What do you see?"

"Iceberg right ahead."[8]

Two passengers stay fit in the *Titanic*'s gym during the journey. The passengers had enjoyed the first few days of a wonderful journey, but late at night on April 14, many woke up to find out that the *Titanic* had struck an iceberg.

THE IMPOSSIBLE HAPPENS

THE OFFICERS ON THE TITANIC'S BRIDGE reacted very quickly.

"Iceberg right ahead!" Junior Officer James Moody repeated to First Officer William Murdoch.

"Hard-a-starboard," Murdoch quickly ordered. The quartermaster, the sailor at the ship's wheel, spun the wheel hard to the right until it would turn no more.[1]

Seconds later, Murdoch ordered the engine room to stop and reverse the engines. This was done to slow the ship's movement toward the iceberg. Preparing for the worst, Murdoch also hit the switch that closed the watertight doors to the hull compartments. As the officers on the bridge and the men in the engine room waited, the *Titanic* slowly turned.[2]

But the ship had been going too fast. Its speed made it impossible to stop the giant vessel before it reached the iceberg. The ship was also

Frederick Fleet, pictured here in 1912, had warned the officers on the bridge about an iceberg in the distance. In the crow's nest, Fleet braced himself for a collision as the ship steamed toward the iceberg.

not turning fast enough. The order to stop and reverse engines made the ship's steering more sluggish. If the engines had only been slowed, rather than reversed, the ship would have actually turned faster.

In the crow's nest, Fleet and Lee braced themselves for a collision. Several large chunks of ice fell onto the ship's decks as the *Titanic* brushed along the iceberg and drifted onward to a stop minutes later. Crew members on the deck were relieved. The ship's bow, or forward section, appeared to have missed the iceberg.[3]

But many of those elsewhere in the ship knew better. Passengers and crew in different parts of the ship either felt a strong shock or heard a scraping noise. The *Titanic* had struck a part of the iceberg below the waterline. Engineers Fred Barrett and James Hesketh were working in the number six boiler room near the front of the ship. Suddenly, the right-side wall of their room crashed open and water gushed in. Hesketh escaped the flood of seawater in the room just before the huge, watertight door slammed shut, sealing the room off from the rest of the ship. Barrett used the emergency escape ladder. The two men were safe for the moment. But the damage to the *Titanic* was more serious than a single hole in a single compartment.

A hard, jagged piece of ice had cut into the lower part of the bow as the ship passed by. It had left a line of holes and crumpled steel along a three-hundred-foot stretch of the hull. Cold seawater was rushing into the number one hold, number two hold, number three hold, number six boiler room, and number five boiler room.

"What have we struck?" asked Captain Smith when he stepped onto the bridge.

"An iceberg, sir," First Officer Murdoch replied. He explained that he had turned the ship, cut the engines, and closed the watertight doors.[4]

The collision had lasted only ten seconds, but the wound the iceberg had inflicted was fatal. The water flowing into the forward portion of the ship belowdecks could not be stopped.

The *Titanic*'s chief designer, Thomas Andrews, was unaware that anything had happened until he heard a knock at his cabin door. A crewman told him to report quickly to the bridge. When Andrews arrived, Captain Smith informed him of the collision. He asked Andrews to accompany him on an inspection of the damage. Their inspection of the shocking scene belowdecks at the ship's forward area lasted less than ten minutes. The compartments were flooding, and Andrews slowly realized that the watertight doors were not going to stop the inflow of water. The men returned to the bridge, where their discussion was brief.

The iceberg had cut a gash so long that it was filling the front five compartments with water. The watertight doors in boiler rooms six and five went only as high as the ship's E deck. As the weight of the water pulled the front of the ship down, the water from the number six boiler room would flow into number five. This would pull the ship even lower, causing the water to flow into the number four boiler room. It would then flow into number three, then number two, and so on.

Andrews's conclusion was grim. There was nothing they could do to change the ship's fate. It was already certain. The *Titanic* was doomed.

"How long have we?" Captain Smith asked.

"An hour and a half," Andrews replied. "Possibly two. Not much longer."

Wasting no time, Captain Smith immediately mobilized his crew. "Uncover the boats," he ordered.[5]

The *Titanic*'s chief designer, Thomas Andrews, informed Captain Edward Smith that the ship had less than two hours before it sank. The ship's officers and crew had to immediately prepare the lifeboats. This photo shows the *Titanic*'s officers. Standing left-to-right are Herbert McElroy, Charles Lightoller, Herbert Pitman, Joseph Boxhall, Harold Lowe, and seated left-to-right are James Moody, Henry Wilde, Captain Smith, and First Officer Murdoch.

The ship's general alarm was never sounded. The alarm might have caused a mad panic among the passengers that would have made abandoning the ship more difficult. Instead, officers were sent through the ship to inform the rest of the crew of the collision. Stewards walked through the decks, telling passengers, many of whom were in bed, to dress and put on lifejackets. When the ship's position was calculated, Captain Smith delivered it to John Phillips and Harold Bride, the ship's wireless operators.

"We've struck an iceberg," Smith told them. "Send the call for assistance." Phillips and Bride went to work at once.[6]

Details about the ship's damage were not communicated to every crew member. Some stewards were unable to tell passengers exactly what had happened, and many passengers could not believe there was any real danger. The result was confusion about the urgency to get to the lifeboats.

At 12:10 A.M., passenger Elizabeth Shutes saw a ship's officer and asked if there was any danger.

"No," the officer responded, trying to avoid the spread of panic. But as he went further down the corridor, Shutes overheard him say to another crewman, "I think we can keep the water out a bit longer."[7]

Margaret "Molly" Brown heard the news that they were to get ready to abandon ship. After traveling in Egypt, she had a collection of important Egyptian relics in her cabin. Just before leaving, Molly grabbed one of the pieces. It was a small figurine. She took it with her for good luck.

Ruth Becker was only twelve years old. She was traveling with her mother and younger brother and sister. A steward told them to get ready to leave quickly.

"Do we have time to dress?" Ruth's mother asked.

"You have time for nothing," the steward replied. "Put on your lifejackets and come up to the boat deck." Ruth helped her mother dress her baby brother and sister. They were in such a hurry they forgot to put on their lifejackets.[8]

At that moment, few, if any, passengers knew the grim truth about the lifeboats. There were not nearly enough. The sixteen wooden lifeboats and the four collapsible boats on board could keep a total of 1,178 people afloat. But there were 2,208 aboard the *Titanic*. That meant that 1,030 people would be without lifeboats. Strangely, the law did not require the ship to carry enough boats for everyone.

Anyone who tried to escape the ship by jumping into the water with or without a lifejacket would freeze in a short time in the icy waters of the North Atlantic. Unless another ship came, those without a lifeboat would not survive.

Despite the fact that the crew had never conducted a lifeboat drill on the *Titanic*, they were orderly in getting the boats ready to be loaded. At 12:25 A.M., nearly an hour after the collision, Captain Smith gave the order to start loading the lifeboats with women and children.

First Officer Murdoch was in charge of the boats on the ship's port, or left side, while Second Officer Charles Lightoller was responsible for the boats on the starboard, or right, side. When Lightoller made the first call for women and children to get into lifeboat No. 6, some passengers were still not convinced of the danger. They felt certain that rescue ships would arrive long before the *Titanic* went under, if it ever went under at all. John Jacob Astor, the richest man on the ship, was not ready to depend on a wooden lifeboat for his survival.

"We are safer here than in that little boat," he said to people standing around him.[9]

Louis and Michel Navratil of Nice, France, sit on their mother's lap for this photograph taken after they survived the *Titanic* shipwreck. Captain Smith first ordered the lifeboats to be filled with women and children, but some women refused to leave without their husbands.

The ship's small orchestra had set up their instruments on the boat deck and were playing music. Their presence helped add a sense of calm to what was happening on the deck.

A few of the women refused to get into a lifeboat without their husbands. When no more women came forward, a few couples and a few other men were allowed to get in. At 12:45 A.M., boat No. 7 on the ship's port side became the first boat to be lowered into the water. It was large enough to carry sixty-five people. But because of confusion, and many passengers' reluctance to leave the *Titanic,* the boat was lowered with only twenty-eight people in it.

Up on the ship's bridge, Fourth Officer Joseph Boxhall ordered quartermaster George Rowe to begin firing distress rockets. Rowe fired the first rocket, which scattered twelve brilliant flares into the sky. Rowe fired a new rocket every five minutes so that any passing ships could spot the *Titanic.*

At about the same time, Boxhall observed the faint lights of a ship passing within five or six miles of the *Titanic.* He used a Morse code lamp to send flashes of a distress code to the other ship. But the ship slowly turned and vanished over the horizon. More than an hour after the collision, there was no rescue in sight.

Wireless operators John Phillips and Harold Bride continued to send out calls for assistance. A number of ships had responded, but they were all too far away to help the *Titanic. Carpathia* was the closest ship to respond. Its wireless operator tapped out a message that it was fifty-eight miles away and heading full steam to the *Titanic*'s rescue.

But the *Carpathia* would not arrive in time. The *Titanic*'s bow was already dipping far into the water. The tilt of the decks was growing steeper. Those who had doubts earlier could now see that the mighty ship was really sinking. Passengers began to crowd around the lifeboats. They started loading into the lifeboats in larger numbers.

Many of the third-class passengers were kept belowdecks to keep the boat decks from getting too crowded. This meant that only first- and second-class passengers were getting into the lifeboats. Third-class

A lifeboat from the *Titanic* is photographed as it approaches the *Carpathia*. Despite the crew's best effort to keep loading the lifeboats in an orderly fashion, it was a difficult task. Several lifeboats were launched only half-full. As panic spread through the ship, it was clear that hundreds of people would go down with the *Titanic*.

passengers were not. As the ship's decks tilted further, the ship's doom became clear to everyone, and panic was brewing belowdecks.

Crewmen continued to load the boats with mostly women and children. Molly Brown was walking away from the deck area when she was grabbed and dropped into boat No. 6.

Wealthy businessman Isidor Straus decided that he would stay with the big ship and leave space for others on the lifeboats. Crewmen and others on deck encouraged his wife to get into one of the boats.

"We have been living together for many years," she told her husband. "Where you go, I go."[10]

The wife of French novelist Jacques Futrelle also would not get into a lifeboat.

"For God's sake, go!" her husband told her. "It's your last chance! Go!" As she continued to protest, an officer decided the matter by forcing her into a lifeboat.[11]

Twelve-year-old Ruth Becker watched her younger brother and sister get loaded into boat No. 11. The crew suddenly began to lower the boat.

"Oh, let me go with my children!" Ruth's mother screamed, and jumped into the boat with them. Ruth was left standing on the deck.[12]

Her mother called back to Ruth to get into another lifeboat. Ruth went down the deck to the next lifeboat. She asked the officer if she could get in. The officer picked her up and put her in a boat. It was so full that she had to stand up. As the crowded boat neared the water, another boat was lowered nearly on top of them. A man in Ruth's boat pulled out a knife and cut their boat free from the ropes. The lifeboat pushed away from the side of the ship just seconds before the other one would have landed on top of it.

By 1:30 A.M., panic was spreading. The *Titanic*'s bow was submerged. The decks continued to slant toward the water. Many people were still aboard and only a few lifeboats were left. The *Titanic*'s time was running out.

CHAPTER FOUR

SWALLOWED BY THE SEA

PANIC AND DISORDER GREW AMONG THE *Titanic*'s passengers. They became more anxious to get into the lifeboats. Fifth Officer Harold Lowe drew his revolver. He fired three warning shots along the outside of the ship. He wanted to keep passengers from crowding against the remaining boats.

By 1:50 A.M., the ship's sixteen wooden lifeboats were away. Only the four collapsible boats reamined. Several crewmen began loading collapsible boat D. Second Officer Charles Lightoller ordered them to lock arms and form a circle around the boat. Only women and children were allowed to pass through and climb aboard.

At another part of the ship, the wealthy American industrialist Benjamin Guggenheim and his aide Victor Giglio emerged from their cabins. They had taken off their sweaters and lifejackets and changed into tuxedos and ties.

***Titanic* survivor John B. Thayer and L. P. Skidmore drew this illustration of the colossal ship sinking immediately after the rescue of the survivors.**

"We've dressed in our best," Guggenheim said, "and are prepared to go down like gentlemen."[1]

At about 2:00 A.M., Captain Smith told the wireless operators that they were relieved of duty. After the captain left, however, Phillips and Bride kept working for several more minutes. Captain Smith relieved every crew member he saw on his way back to the bridge. Standing on the *Titanic*'s bridge, he waited for its plunge into the sea.

Water flooded up through the lower decks. Passengers hurried away from the rising water. The small orchestra on the boat deck played their last song, "Nearer, My God, to Thee." Then they broke up to await their fates.

The attempt to launch collapsible boat B ended when the *Titanic*'s sinking bow plunged Second Officer Lightoller and others into the water. Swimming in the icy water, they tried to climb onto the overturned boat.

The ship's stern tilted into the air, slowly rising higher above the water. Boilers within the ship exploded, killing many crewmen and passengers who were still below. As the ship sank deeper into the water, waves passed by, sweeping people out to sea.

More than 1,500 people were still onboard, and no rescue ships were in sight. But the *Titanic*'s moments were numbered. The stern rose higher and higher above the sea as water flooded the bow. From her lifeboat, Ruth Becker watched the *Titanic*'s final moments.

"I could look back and see this ship, and the decks were just lined with people looking over," she later said. "Finally, as the *Titanic* sank faster, the lights died out. You could just see the stern remaining in an upright position for a couple of minutes. Then . . . it disappeared."[2]

Another passenger, August Wennerstrom, floated a safe distance away. He watched the scene from his collapsible boat.

"It was horrible," he said, "but at the same time, in a way that I am unable to explain, wonderfully dramatic."[3]

Helen Candee, in another lifeboat, also witnessed the end of the mighty ship.

Molly Brown appears in this photo after the *Carpathia* arrived in New York following the *Titanic* shipwreck. While in lifeboat No. 6, Brown insisted that they row toward any surviving swimmers, but no rescues were made.

"At the last," she said, "the end of the world . . . she went down with an awful grating."[4]

The massive ocean liner had vanished into the sea. Hundreds of people were left floating in the freezing water. A handful of men climbed onto collapsible boat B. A few others were hauled out of the water by people in lifeboats. But most were just left in the water.

Molly Brown insisted that her lifeboat, No. 6, row toward the surviving swimmers. She wanted to rescue as many people as possible before they froze. But crewman Robert Hitchens and passenger Arthur Peuchen were arguing over who was in command of the lifeboat. Hitchens would not listen to Molly's pleas. Frederick Fleet, the lookout who had originally spotted the iceberg, was the only other man on board to work the oars. Molly showed the other women how to row. But many of them were afraid they would all be dumped into the water if they tried to rescue other people. As arguments continued among Brown, Hitchens, and Peuchen, the women worked the oars to keep warm. But no rescues were made.[5]

The cries of people in the water gradually quieted, then stopped. They had survived the actual sinking but slowly froze to death in the water. Of the hundreds who had jumped into the water when the ship sank, only twelve survived.

It was nearly two hours before a ship, the *Carpathia,* arrived to pull the survivors aboard to safety. The *Carpathia* shot flares into the sky to alert other ships that the survivors had been found. Many of the lifeboats were close to sinking by the time the *Carpathia* got to them.

Second Officer Lightoller and wireless operator Harold Bride were among the thirty men who spent the night clinging to the top of collapsible boat B. A few of the men had frozen and quietly slid into the water during the night. Their boat was so low in the water that Lightoller was afraid the *Carpathia* would not see them. He pulled out his pocket whistle and blew on it several times. The ship eventually came to rescue them. Officer Lightoller was the last *Titanic* survivor to climb aboard the *Carpathia*.[6]

When the search for survivors ended at about 8:00 A.M., the *Carpathia*'s crew had pulled only 705 *Titanic* crew members and passengers from the icy Atlantic. The rest, 1,503 people, were dead. Wireless reports from the *Carpathia* sent the news back to England and ahead to New York, where the ship would arrive in three days. Newspapers around the world gave banner headlines to the tragic story.

On the evening of April 18, 1912, the *Carpathia* arrived in New York harbor, carrying the *Titanic*'s survivors. Even though it was the middle of a rainstorm, thirty thousand people were waiting along the docks.

The White Star Line hired a ship from Nova Scotia to search for bodies at the site of the sinking, an area about 500 miles southeast of Newfoundland. After two weeks, the crew had pulled 328 bodies from the water. About half of the bodies were identified and claimed by loved ones for burial. Some were so badly decomposed, or decayed, that they could not be identified. They were buried at sea after a service by a clergyman on the ship. The remaining 150 unclaimed bodies were buried in three cemeteries in Halifax, Nova Scotia.

The survivors went on with their lives, but none would ever forget this disaster. They were often asked to retell the stories of their experiences during the sinking. Molly Brown was interviewed by many newspaper reporters after arriving in New York. Responding to the question of how she survived the disaster, Brown told one reporter she was unsinkable. This is how she became known as "the unsinkable Mrs. Brown."

Immediately after the tragedy, a series of investigations began. By learning exactly what went wrong with the *Titanic,* it was hoped that such a disaster at sea would never happen again.

Investigations by both the United States Senate and the British Board of Trade agreed that the construction of the hull compartments was flawed. The hull compartments should not have allowed water to spill upward into the higher decks.

"All the News That's Fit to Print."

The New York Times.

NEW YORK, TUESDAY, APRIL 16, 1912.—TWENTY-FOUR PAGES, ONE CENT

TITANIC SINKS FOUR HOURS AFTER HITTING ICEBERG; 866 RESCUED BY CARPATHIA, PROBABLY 1250 PERISH; ISMAY SAFE, MRS. ASTOR MAYBE, NOTED NAMES MISSING

Col. Astor and Bride, Isidor Straus and Wife, and Maj. Butt Aboard.

"RULE OF SEA" FOLLOWED

Women and Children Put Over in Lifeboats and Are Supposed to be Safe on Carpathia.

PICKED UP AFTER 8 HOURS

Vincent Astor Calls at White Star Office for News of His Father and Leaves Weeping.

FRANKLIN HOPEFUL ALL DAY

Manager of the Line Insisted Titanic Was Unsinkable Even After She Had Gone Down.

HEAD OF THE LINE ABOARD

J. Bruce Ismay Making First Trip on Gigantic Ship That Was to Surpass All Others.

The admission that the Titanic, the biggest steamship in the world, had been sunk by an iceberg and had gone to the bottom of the Atlantic, probably carrying more than 1,400 of her passengers and crew with her, was made at the White Star Line offices, 9 Broadway, at 8:20 o'clock last night. Then P. A. S. Franklin, Vice President and General Manager of the Interna-

The Lost Titanic Being Towed Out of Belfast Harbor.

PARTIAL LIST OF THE SAVED.

Biggest Liner Plunges to the Bottom at 2:20 A. M.

RESCUERS THERE TOO LATE

Except to Pick Up the Few Hundreds Who Took to the Lifeboats.

WOMEN AND CHILDREN FIRST

Cunarder Carpathia Rushing to New York with the Survivors.

SEA SEARCH FOR OTHERS

The California Stands By on Chance of Picking Up Other Boats or Rafts.

OLYMPIC SENDS THE NEWS

Only Ship to Flash Wireless Messages to Shore After the Disaster.

LATER REPORT SAVES 866.

BOSTON, April 15.—A wireless message picked up late to-night, relayed from the Olympic, says that the Carpathia is on her way to New York with [illegible] passengers from the steamer Titanic aboard. They are mostly women and children, the message said, and it concluded: "Grave fears are felt for the safety of the balance of the

This headline reporting the *Titanic* disaster appeared on the front page of the *New York Times* on April 16, 1912. Investigations into the shipwreck resulted in a number of new laws for ships regarding lifeboats and other emergency protocol.

The British investigation was not critical of Captain Smith. However, the American investigators felt that Captain Smith had been careless. They felt he should have slowed or stopped the ship after receiving the repeated ice warnings. In fact, Captain Smith had increased the ship to almost full speed after the warnings.

Also, no special lookout had been ordered when the *Titanic* entered the area where icebergs had been reported. There was not even a pair of binoculars in the crow's nest.

The two investigations also found fault with Captain Stanley Lord of the ocean liner *Californian*. The *Californian* may have been the ship that Fourth Officer Boxhall saw passing by about an hour after the collision. Investigators found that crewmen aboard the *Californian* had seen all eight of the *Titanic*'s distress rockets, and reported them to their captain. But Captain Lord did nothing. He did not even order anyone to turn on the wireless machine to listen for a distress call.

During the hours after the collision, the *Californian* was the only ship that passed near the *Titanic*. If Captain Lord and his crew had responded to the *Titanic*'s rockets, most of those aboard the *Titanic* would likely have been saved.[7]

Both investigations found the White Star Line unprepared for an emergency on the *Titanic*. The company should have had more than two times the number of lifeboats available on the ship. Also, the crew was never required to conduct a lifeboat drill during the trip. The crew's lack of practice added to the confusion as people were boarding the lifeboats.

The investigations into the *Titanic*'s sinking resulted in a number of new laws. Every ship at sea now had to have a radio operator on duty at all times. This was done to keep track of navigation warnings. In addition, the United States created the International Ice Patrol. This patrol keeps a constant count of icebergs and reports their positions to nearby ships. Probably the most important new law required all ships to carry enough lifeboats for all crew members and passengers on board.[8]

The investigations were over by the middle of 1912. But nothing would ever end the public's interest in the *Titanic*.

CHAPTER FIVE

A LEGENDARY TRAGEDY

MORE THAN A CENTURY LATER, the story of the *Titanic* still captivates the public. Over the many years since the ship was lost, it has lived on in many different forms of art, literature, and film.

The most famous film adaptation is *Titanic,* released in 1997. The story at the center of the movie was a fictionalized romance between Jack Dawson, played by Leonardo DiCaprio, and Rose DeWitt Bukater, played by Kate Winslet. Directed by James Cameron with a production budget of $200 million, the film went on to gross more than $1.8 billion worldwide.[1] More than a decade later, Cameron remade the film in 3-D for re-release in 2012—one hundred years after the sinking of the real-life ship.[2]

Cameron's interest in the *Titanic* began while he was doing research for another film, *The Abyss.*[3] It was about this same time, in 1985, that the wreckage of the *Titanic* was discovered by Dr. Robert Ballard and his crew. Ballard's exploration revealed that the *Titanic* had broken in

The tragic story of the *Titanic* has been featured in art, literature, and film. It was most popularly portrayed in the 1997 movie *Titanic*. This photo depicts a scene in which the film's stars, Leonardo DiCaprio and Kate Winslet, run through the interior of the ship as it sinks.

half before sinking. The two sections were found at the ocean floor almost two thousand feet apart.[4]

Ten years later, Cameron filmed footage of the wreck for use in his famous film. Cameron described the experience of filming the wreckage as "sort of like going to Mecca" and "getting religion." He went on to say:

> Working around the wreck for so much time, you get such a strong sense of the profound sadness and injustice of it, and the message of it. You think, "There probably aren't going to be many filmmakers who go to *Titanic*. There may never be another one—maybe a documentarian." So it sort of becomes a great mantle of responsibility to convey the emotional message of it.[5]

While many recovered artifacts from the ship have been put on display in shows and exhibitions over the years, the wreckage itself will not likely survive much longer. Dr. Henrietta Mann observed: "In 1995, I was predicting that *Titanic* had another 30 years. . . . But I think it's deteriorating much faster than that now. Eventually there will be nothing left but a rust stain."[6]

On May 31, 2009, Millvina Dean, the last *Titanic* survivor, died at the age of ninety-seven. As a two-month-old infant aboard the ship, she was bundled in a mail sack and lowered into a lifeboat. Though her mother and brother survived with her, her father, Bertram Dean, was among those who died. Ms. Dean believed that her family's working-class background played a part in her father's death. The Dean family had been traveling in third class (steerage). Ms. Dean was among those who believed that upper-class passengers were shown favoritism in boarding lifeboats.

"It couldn't happen nowadays, and it's so wrong, so unjust," she said in an interview just a month before she died.[7]

A view of the *Titanic*'s bow resting on the bottom of the North Atlantic Ocean. Salvage crews have searched the wreckage of the *Titanic* several times, studying the ship's remains and recovering priceless artifacts.

In her final years, Dean struggled to pay the costs of living in a nursing home. James Cameron, Leonardo DiCaprio, and Kate Winslet all contributed to the Millvina Fund to help Dean pay her bills.[8]

In 2011, the centennial anniversary of the launching of the *Titanic* was celebrated in Belfast. At 12:13 P.M., a single flare was fired as all the ships blew their horns and the crowd applauded for 62 seconds—the exact time it took the *Titanic* to roll down her slipway in 1911. In attendance was Susie Millar, great-granddaughter of one of the ship's engineers. She said, "Today is a day when we can celebrate *Titanic*. When it comes to next year, 2012, it's a time for commemoration and reflection and obviously the sadness of what happened to the ship, but

On display in the traveling *Titanic* exhibit on March 23, 2006, is this piece of sheet music for the song "Put Your Arms Around Me Honey" that the doomed musicians played aboard the sinking ship. This precious artifact, along with hundreds of others recovered from the wreckage of the ship, keeps the *Titanic*'s memory alive.

now in 2011 we can look at the ship as a brilliant piece of engineering and celebrate the achievement of Belfast in building that ship."[9]

A one-hundredth-anniversary cruise was planned for 2012. Fred Olsen Cruise Lines, whose parent company was Harland and Wolff, would provide their ship, the *Balmoral,* for the trip. It was scheduled to carry the same number of passengers as the *Titanic* had (1,316) and follow the same route used one hundred years later. Miles Morgan, managing director of the cruise, declared:

> The whole voyage will be steeped in *Titanic* history. The food served will match the sumptuous menus on the original voyage; the entertainment will include music and dancing in the style featured in those glorious times and there will be a chance to hear firsthand from historians who have studied the *Titanic* story. . . . The fascination for the *Titanic* is as strong as ever.[10]

CHAPTER NOTES

CHAPTER 1. "ICEBERG RIGHT AHEAD!"

1. Charles Pellegrino, *Her Name,* Titanic (New York: McGraw Hill Publishing Company, 1988), p. 101.
2. John P. Eaton and Charles A. Haas, Titanic*: Triumph and Tragedy* (New York: W. W. Norton & Company, 1994), p. 137.

CHAPTER 2. THE BIGGEST AND FINEST

1. John P. Eaton and Charles A. Haas, Titanic*: Triumph and Tragedy* (New York: W. W. Norton & Company, 1994), pp. 20–31.
2. Robert D. Ballard, *Exploring the* Titanic (Toronto, Ontario: Madison Publishing Inc., 1988), p. 10.
3. Beverly McMillan and Stanley Lehrer, Titanic*: Fortune and Fate* (New York: Simon and Schuster, 1998), p. 16.
4. Walter Lord, *A Night to Remember* (New York: Bantam Books, 1955), p. 26.
5. Ballard, p. 11.
6. McMillan and Lehrer, p. 27.
7. Eaton and Haas, pp. 114–115.
8. Ibid., p. 137.

CHAPTER 3. THE IMPOSSIBLE HAPPENS

1. John P. Eaton and Charles A. Haas, Titanic*: Triumph and Tragedy* (New York: W. W. Norton & Company, 1994), p. 137.
2. Robert D. Ballard, *Exploring the* Titanic (Toronto, Ontario: Madison Publishing Inc., 1988), p. 20.
3. Charles Pellegrino, *Her Name,* Titanic (New York: McGraw Hill Publishing Company, 1988), p. 21.
4. Walter Lord, *A Night to Remember* (New York: Bantam Books, 1955), p. 8.
5. Eaton and Haas, p. 143.
6. Wyn Craig Wade, *The* Titanic*: End of a Dream* (New York: Rawson, Wade Publishers, Inc., 1979), p. 31.

7. Eaton and Haas, p. 145.
8. Ballard, p. 23.
9. Lord, p. 43.
10. Pellegrino, p. 172.
11. Eaton and Haas, p. 152.
12. Beverly McMillan and Stanley Lehrer, Titanic*: Fortune and Fate* (New York: Simon and Schuster, 1998), p. 82.

CHAPTER 4. SWALLOWED BY THE SEA

1. Beverly McMillan and Stanley Lehrer, Titanic*: Fortune and Fate* (New York: Simon and Schuster, 1998), p. 41.
2. Robert D. Ballard, *Exploring the* Titanic (Toronto, Ontario: Madison Publishing Inc., 1988), p. 29.
3. Wyn Craig Wade, *The* Titanic*: End of a Dream* (New York: Rawson, Wade Publishers, Inc., 1979), pp. 213–214.
4. Ibid., p. 214.
5. Walter Lord, *A Night to Remember* (New York: Bantam Books, 1955), pp. 128–129.
6. John P. Eaton and Charles A. Haas, Titanic*: Triumph and Tragedy* (New York: W. W. Norton & Company, 1994), p. 179.
7. Wade, pp. 237–241.
8. Eaton and Haas, pp. 259–275.

CHAPTER 5. A LEGENDARY TRAGEDY

1. "*Titanic*," *The Numbers*, 1997–2011, <http://www.the-numbers.com/movies/1997/TITAN.php> (July 29, 2011).
2. "Paramount Pictures, Twentieth Century Fox and Lightstorm Entertainment to Set Sail Again with James Cameron's Oscar®-Winning "Titanic" with a Worldwide 3D Re-Release on April 6, 2012," Paramount Pictures, May 19, 2011, <http://www.paramount.com/news/press-releases/paramount-pictures-twentieth-century-fox-and-lightstorm-entertainment-to-set-sail-again-with-james-c> (July 29, 2011).
3. Rick Schultz, "James Cameron Tells the Astonishing Story of *Titanic*, His Breathtaking Labor of Love," *The Director's Chair*, n.d., <http://industrycentral.net/director_interviews/JC01.HTM> (July 20, 2011).

4. Robert D. Ballard, *Exploring the* Titanic (Toronto, Ontario: Madison Publishing Inc., 1988), pp. 38–60.

5. Schultz, "James Cameron Tells the Astonishing Story of *Titanic,* His Breathtaking Labor of Love."

6. Craig Johnson, "New Metal-Eating Bacteria Found on *Titanic,*" *CNN.com,* December 11, 2010, <http://news.blogs.cnn.com/2010/12/11/new-metal-eating-bacteria-found-on-titanic/?hpt=C2> (July 20, 2011).

7. John F. Burns, "Millvina Dean, *Titanic*'s Last Survivor, Dies at 97," *New York Times,* June 1, 2009, <http://www.nytimes.com/2009/06/01/world/europe/01dean.html> (July 29, 2011).

8. Ibid.

9. "*Titanic* Launch 100th Anniversary Marked by Belfast Flare," *The Telegraph,* May 31, 2011, <http://www.telegraph.co.uk/news/uknews/northernireland/8547713/Titanic-launch-100th-anniversary-marked-by-Belfast-flare.html> (July 29, 2011).

10. Charles Starmer-Smith, "*Titanic* Cruise to Mark Anniversary of Ship's Fateful Voyage," *The Telegraph,* April 14, 2009, <http://www.telegraph.co.uk/travel/cruises/cruise-news/5154038/Titanic-cruise-to-mark-anniversary-of-ships-fateful-voyage.html> (July 29, 2011).

GLOSSARY

bow—The front end of a ship.

bridge—An elevated room or structure toward the front of the ship where crew members have a clear view ahead, and from which the ship is navigated.

CQD—A Morse code signal used in the early days of wireless communication. It meant "Come, Quick, Danger."

crow's nest—A lookout platform high on a ship's mast.

dry dock—A dock out of the water that is used for the construction and repair of ships.

hull—The frame or body of a ship.

lifeboat—A boat carried aboard a larger ship for use in emergencies.

maiden voyage—The first voyage of a new ship.

Morse code—A code invented by Samuel Morse, made up of a series of dots and dashes to represent letters of the alphabet. The messages could be sent by tapping out sounds on a radio or by flashing a Morse lamp.

Morse lamp—A lamp used to flash signals in Morse code.

port—The left side of a ship, as seen when facing forward.

starboard—The right side of a ship, as seen when facing forward.

stern—The rear end of a ship.

steward—A ship's crew member who attends to the needs of passengers.

wireless—An early form of radio communication that carried electronic code bleeps but not voice communication.

FURTHER READING

BOOKS

Benoit, Peter. *The* Titanic *Disaster*. New York: Children's Press, 2011.

Brown, Don. *All Stations! Distress!: April 15, 1912, The Day the* Titanic *Sank*. New York: Roaring Book Press, 2008.

Burlingame, Jeff. *The* Titanic *Tragedy*. New York: Marshall Cavendish Benchmark, 2012.

McPherson, Stephanie Sammartino. *Iceberg Right Ahead! The Sinking of the* Titanic. Minneapolis, Minn.: Twenty-First Century Books, 2012.

Pipe, Jim. *The* Titanic. Buffalo, N.Y.: Firefly Books, 2007.

INTERNET ADDRESSES

Encyclopedia Titanica
<http://www.encyclopedia-titanica.org/>

RMS *Titanic* Home Page
<http://www.rmstitanic.net/>

Titanic Historical Society
<http://www.titanic1.org/>

INDEX